ROMANTIC

ROMANTIC

Poems

MARK
CALLANAN

FIRST EDITION

Library and Archives Canada Cataloguing in Publication

Title: Romantic / Mark Callanan.
Names: Callanan, Mark, 1979- author.
Description: Poems.
Identifiers: Canadiana (print) 20210225793 | Canadiana (ebook) 20210225823 | ISBN 9781771964456 (softcover) | ISBN 9781771964463 (ebook)
Classification: LCC PS8555.A497 R66 2021 | DDC C811/.6—dc23

Edited by Luke Hathaway
Copyedited by Emily Donaldson
Text and cover designed by Gordon Robertson

Canada Council for the Arts Conseil des Arts du Canada
ONTARIO CREATES | ONTARIO CRÉATIF
Canada
ONTARIO ARTS COUNCIL
CONSEIL DES ARTS DE L'ONTARIO
an Ontario government agency
un organisme du gouvernement de l'Ontario
ArtsNL
NEWFOUNDLAND AND LABRADOR ARTS COUNCIL

Published with the generous assistance of the Canada Council for the Arts, which last year invested $153 million to bring the arts to Canadians throughout the country, and the financial support of the Government of Canada. Biblioasis also acknowledges the support of the Ontario Arts Council (OAC), an agency of the Government of Ontario, which last year funded 1,709 individual artists and 1,078 organizations in 204 communities across Ontario, for a total of $52.1 million, and the contribution of the Government of Ontario through the Ontario Book Publishing Tax Credit and Ontario Creates.

PRINTED AND BOUND IN CANADA

for
Anita Best

&

in memory of
Edythe Goodridge
(née Ryan)

And, indeed it is a very pleasant thing for to ride forth in the dawning of a Springtime day. For then the little birds do sing their sweetest song, all joining in one joyous medley, whereof one may scarce tell one note from another, so multitudinous is that pretty roundelay; then do the growing things of the earth smell the sweetest in the freshness of the early daytime—the fair flowers, the shrubs, and the blossoms upon the trees; then doth the dew bespangle all the sward as with an incredible multitude of jewels of various colours; then is all the world sweet and clean and new, as though it had been fresh created for him who came to roam abroad so early in the morning.

— Howard Pyle
The Story of King Arthur and His Knights

There was a time when meadow, grove, and stream,
The earth, and every common sight,
            To me did seem
        Apparelled in celestial light,
The glory and the freshness of a dream.
It is not now as it hath been of yore;—
        Turn wheresoe'er I may,
            By night or day,
The things which I have seen I now can see no more.

— William Wordsworth
"Ode: Intimations of Immortality
from Recollections of Early Childhood"

CONTENTS

ROMANTIC

ARCANE

It was a coin trick
with a magic cabinet.
You waved a wand
that made a man appear
to walk across a screen,
drawing out a string
of foes that issued
from the lines of code
concealed within
the program's sleeve.

Sleight of hand became
the new heroics.
The real, transmuted,
held us in its spell.
So we practiced the arcane
art of changing
what was base about us.
We were golden, then,
and took the shape
of anything we chose.

SHOTGUN

We would all try to call it
first in those days when few
of us had a valid license
and to come second meant
the hatchback's cramped
backseat, crammed in
like reluctant children
we were trying not to be,
fleeing childhood's confines,
its tailgating memories:
pang of the sun-charged
buckle on a bare leg,
car trips through
endless outports
to name the face
of some distant relative
we had never seen.

Better to be, if not
in the driver's seat,
then passive viewer
as the windshield
screened the road ahead
like a dash cam's
live feed. Beyond
reproach or collision,
we cut in where we did
not belong, laughed
too loud, made obscene
gestures at other drivers
on a strip-lit bypass
that skirted the periphery
of the town we were born in.
Cigarettes and coffee. Gas
when required. We prowled

our territory like hunters,
game for anything,
so that when my friend
unpacked a twelve
gauge from his parents'
pitted Skylark, it was
no big thing. An access
road just outside town.
I jumped a culvert, hung
a pop can on a spruce
tree near the shoulder.
The day was dying.
Crows gathered
on the highest branches,
elemental, perched exactly.
He took aim. I claimed
the driver's seat and waited.

CLICHÉ

Even our delusions are guilty
of striking the dominant
pose. Years ago, you were
nobody if you weren't
the big J.C. hoofing it
down St. John's streets
in a t-shirt in January,
spreading the good news
with venereal efficiency,
sparing fellow citizens
their handful of venial sins.
Came a time, the web
of self-delusion set its net
worldwide. Dial up. Early
Internet. *You* remember.
Then the tone switched
from sacred to paranoid:
G-men in surveillance vans;
tapped phones; web traffic
monitored. Tinfoil
capped the era with
a new trend in apparel.
Now, I'm told, they're
returning to the old
tropes, visions and
revisions of Christ
talking through the buzz
of neon lights, bushes
giving sermons. The sonnet
is making a big comeback,
or might yet, someday.

THE MONITOR

Shielded from disaster in the bunker
of my office, I decrypt static
transmissions from the baby monitor,
a wartime shortwave operator

awake to coded troop movements,
rumours of invasion. No news
is good news, and your breath,
unabated, the best kind of monotony.

Until comes the hitch, the sudden
cry. Then on my feet and
lurching for the door I am

the bearer of bad news en route
with his communiqué, to say
they're coming. They're on their way.

ROMANTIC

Like the Green Knight, stooping
to retrieve his own severed melon
from the stone floor of a banquet
hall where it rolls past startled
courtiers to then catch against a
table leg and stop, I'm fumbling
for an errant thought; without his
flair for theatre, the practised ease
with which he grips a hank of
hair and hoists his head aloft,
as if it is a lantern shedding
light most curious on these noble
faces; without the magic touch
that makes a campy horror stunt
seem plausible and frightening
to its audience: Gawain, the bravest;
the only one of Arthur's knights
to rise up at this boastful guest,
accept his dubious challenge,
then hack the very head off him—
off him who now stands up,
and takes decapitated head in hand
to shake its gory locks, to lavish
on those lords and ladies wine-
red blood decanted from the gourd
that was his head; Gawain, gone
ghostly at the thought of such
a trek through darkened woods,
wherein there lies a chapel,
most foreboding in its aspect.
There will he pursue this quest
to settle up by seeing his own
head chopped off.

But figuratively:
He won't *see* anything, unless one
trusts the doctor, centuries later,
who claimed a freshly severed head
had blinked in answer to its name,
thereby confirming that the body
is vestigial, a survival from the past,
which long since passed the limits
of utility, persisting in existence
as if the fact of one's existence is
the point. It's not. The doctor kept
pursuing this novel line of inquiry,
but in the end, he failed to prove
what happens to a person that has
poured out of the vessel they once
filled; whereas the headless subject
of that first experiment just carried
on his way to be interred or burned,
as befitted his beliefs. I believe
we were done mounting heads on
pikes by then, but truth be told,
my research consists mostly of these
tales, wherein a knight who rides
through darkened woods can end up
hewn apart from all he was.
All this
to say, there's *me* most comfortable
in motley clothes, his jester's job
of playing dumb for royal lols:
a well-trained animal that rolls
fresh paint on walls for clientele
whose living rooms are just so
tired of this tone; but also, there
is *me* apart, who watches passively,
observing how his fingers work
a clavier to make words describe

the quiet parts between the parts
a scribe set down in ink; a *me* so
insubstantial as to float: a vacant,
poorly stitched and half-inflated
bladder of a pig that's kicked free
of the muck by village kids—a lazy
punt that lofts beyond a rooftop,
out of sight; a me that *thinks* it
thought itself to be, and thereby
tips its ostentatious fool's cap
to the doctors and philosophers
both proving that *I am*, at once,
the lawful, reigning monarch of
this throne, and the usurper who
has been removed from all he knows,
doomed to live his life in exile
on this pike pole, at the city gates.

THE HOLD

He's telling me about the livestock-
grade epinephrine he injected in
his buddy's leg—a sudden gust
propelling him from passed out

drunk to *standing like a ship's*
mast in full sail, blown free from
the doldrums of a dozen lagers,
from keeled off on the kitchen floor.

At the summit of a ladder, looking
down at me who's there to keep
its feet from kicking out, he tells
the how and why of it and laughs,

a joke that time between *back*
then and *now* retells. A factory
across the pond. A graveyard
shift spent mixing animal feed

and dosing all the symptoms
of ennui—of a body that's
enlisted in its labour while
the brain, bereft, just churns

itself to fodder. He climbs back
down and passes me the paint.
You slash a bag, fill the hopper.
Then you do it over, he explains,

his arms outstretched like oars mid-
stroke to demonstrate ungainly
bulk, then rifles in his kit bag
for a joint. He lights it, smokes,

and talks of how a mind adrift
on night shifts tends to wander
from its post. So *you curse
yourself* for dereliction,

barking orders at what isn't
mashed on grog already,
imprisoned in the brig below
deck, below the waterline,

where all the cargo's kept.

CUE

What power is it in a pint
or two too many lagers
that turns ungainly pool cues
into burnished rifles?

Best game I ever played
the balls looked doubled
so the task of sinking them
seemed twice the effort.

Yet I almost ran around
the table as I ran the table.
Each crack dispatched
another to the corner

pocket. My opponent
stood agog, worrying
a cube of chalk, impatient
for his cue: the slip,

the flub that meant
the death of something
good. I downed another
beer, shot from the hip.

Then something sank
and something didn't.

HIGHLIGHT REEL

Slow motion is not fair
to those it renders
in near-stasis—not stuck
or frame-by-frame
but close enough
to show the struggle
on their faces: wild swing;
wide shot; reached out
to catch what passed
them by, if only just.
It sees how hard we try,
so much it feels unkind—
so much it feels unkind
to watch them slowly
shake their heads as if
awaking from a dream.

THE SCORE

Television's version had us
spoiled. We, the crowd,
so high up in our
seats the field

appeared a world away.
Without the play-by-
play, it wasn't
even real.

Instead, this distant vision
of a pitcher ridiculed
by chants that
hexed

whatever happened next.
Beer, the organ charge,
a batter yelling
at a call.

We wanted to be lifted up
but couldn't tell just
who was who
or what

had been resolved. I left
exactly as I'd come,
but different
somehow.

STRIKE ZONE

He was tiny, really, a shard
of snapped bat in the box,
squinting at each pitch
that missed its mark,
balking as the pitcher
grimaced, then wound up
and threw too high or low,
while he leaned back
as if to swing and let it
pass. He eyed the outfield
bleachers, a pretend menace,
one speck of dust
from the cloud kicked up
in a close play at home.
But in his eyes it was obvious
that he was brute force
barely contained, forever
waiting on that perfect
pitch that never came,
batting sand from his cleats,
spitting in the dirt,
crossing himself again.

SCIENCE CAMP

Armed with tongue depressors,
newspapers, cardboard, twine,
they built prototypes to break
an egg's fall from on high;
launched homemade rockets
and watched them crash,
entangled in the parachutes
that failed to land them safely
in the field, their wax-form
nose cones blunted on impact;
kept vigil while their model
boats were tossed upon the wave
tank's scaled-down crests and
troughs; and otherwise endured
physics' lessons: how everything
returns to earth, gets wrecked
on the shoals of the universe.

We were failed experiments
ourselves, teenagers falling
down drunk in wooded parks
where glass shards, sloughed
condoms, charred lumber scraps
had washed up from the wreck
of evenings past. We talked
crap about the firmament,
theorized life on other planets.
Absence of proof is not proof
of absence, we repeated, downing
drinks and only half believing it.
Now junior counsellors, we babysat
the children of parents obsessed
by the notion that summers spent
in idleness are summers wasted.

On the final day we took them
to the med school. It pissed
down rain and they got wet,
a pack of sodden animals dripping
puddles in the foyer, easily led
into a lab where steel trays
served donated organs: lungs
butterflied like chicken breasts,
a hand that made a fist
when with a fist you tugged
the tendons like a bell-pull;
pumps and sockets, fuses, pipes:
all the pieces you might use
to build a better prototype.

I don't know what we learned
that day, but something
in my circuits changed,
became rerouted or plain
burnt out by the thought of us
all trudging back through
heavy rain, having seen
a man split open to reveal
the things of which a man is made,
his head and hands and feet
cocooned in orange plastic
bags like autumn leaves,
his penis shrivelled to a stump.
A boy giggled at the sight of it.
I scowled at him but felt
like laughing too, when faced
with what was facing us,
and that's the truth.

THE ODD COUPLETS

He dabbles in a bit of carpentry;
she ponders the chair's asymmetry.

She stays out dancing at a bar;
he uncaps another beer.

He dashes out to grab some milk;
she finds they had some: bottom shelf.

She jogs at least 10K a day;
at night he dreams she's run away.

He read her journal while she slept;
she hates it when he gets half-slapped.

She likes it when he comes home early;
he says he does, but doesn't really.

They married on the tenth of June;
they talk of kids, but not right now.

The flat's too small. There isn't room.

LANCELOT

Because you have no voice,
I'll give you mine. I'm good

like that, and kind. Just
yesterday, I cleared a path

through virgin, pure white
snow—the sidewalk

to my neighbour's step
so that she wouldn't fall.

A nasty spill at her age?
I couldn't bear the thought.

THE RIDER

Ten years old and
skinny, propped
on a gold-flecked
bike that shone like
polished armour,
I popped wheelies:
fought the lightning
strike of panic
in my rearing horse.

By mistake or not,
I let the front
wheel slew off-
course, so when
the bike came
down, it bucked
me overtop, past
the handlebars, past
my errant fantasy

and into this moment
in which I see
the bigger picture:
a boy falling from the sky,
his eyes gone
wild with fear
of what comes next
and what comes next
and what comes after.

SKYLARKING

is what my mother called it
when flights inevitably
stalled: bumped his skull
on the headboard; sprawled
face-first on the hardwood
floor; flipped the bike off
the pallet ramp, embedding
gravel in his palms.
                                        With
children of my own, I know
the cost of *joy whose race*
is just begun; how *sweetest*
songs are those that tell... of
what? *Of saddest thought.*
I should have listened then,
as I am trying to listen now.

CYCLIC

As grass falls
before the blade—
in a suburb with
mature trees and
inflated values
near a department
store that went
straight to video
rentals, then a call
centre, now this
hardware franchise
haunted by the
ghosts of all our
previous failures;
in a neighbourhood
that has its charm
because the maple-
dappled streets
at least are quiet,
the very model of
a modern, sleepy
suburb; unremarkable,
until the evening
news-hour strobes
it red and blue;
but no, the truth
was worse: too late
it was discovered
that the orphaned
Catholic children of

[…]

and so the building
was demolished;
but from the rubble
rose a grocery store
whose produce,
if not great, is passable,
a wholly automated
mist anointing all
those tender heads
of lettuce, leaves
as green as
grass that falls
before the mower
blades I used to pilot
in my headset,
playing Hole
on a cassette tape,
hating all of it—
so will this be razed
for what replaces
it with what
has always been.

VINTAGE

It looked like a fireplace matchstick,
one thin wooden skewer to spark
the dry hut of last week's flyers
thatched with kindling in the grate,

but must have been a long swab
infused with chemicals to scorch
the tender insides of my nostrils,
burning arteries so the blood

that once came unannounced,
running steadily as vintage red
bleeding through cheesecloth
to filter sediment, now ceased.

To come no more, or come only
by blunt force to the face, some
schoolyard misunderstanding,
or comeuppance, interest paid—

a blow that never came, because
I was too clever or too quiet
or too frightened to invite
a corkscrew punch to breach

the homemade plonk I bottle
up. A purifying scarlet gush,
the thin metallic taste I am
no better and no worse than.

LONGSHOREMAN

I'd be like Brando. So I thought.
The hero of the working class,
the brawn who shunts tubs
of snow crab into transport trucks,
letting commerce pass
across his muscled back.
But there I was in the guts
of a factory freezer,
scrawny, freezing, poorly dressed
in cotton gloves and rain gear,
stacking bricks of shrimp
on pallets while my workmates
mocked the deckhand
who told them not to smoke,
pretending that his Russian
accent mistranslated *no*.
I'd written them off
when the biggest of the lot,
seeing me rub my freezing hands
together after every box,
gave me his insulated gloves.
Take these, he said. *They're warmer*.
I quit the following day
and tried to write the screenplay
but found the words
too heavy to be shouldered.
So I took a job in advertising,
hawking hair regeneration cream
to men emasculated by their genes.
To be honest, I was never a contender.

PART OF THE MAIN

You might say a clod washed away
diminishes the whole, the contours
of the land effaced by patient tide,
which knows its tiny contributions
will add up, in time, and thus sub-
tract the coast, but this has all been
said before, and better, long ago.
Carping on about it like the bloody-
minded sea that drags its weight
across beach stones—a washboard
trying to scrub away the stain
of what's been done—won't change
the fact it's easier to turn your back
on everyone. I am content to have
my outraged moment and then sink
into an armchair that won't protest
when I protest against a continent
that is worn down by indifference.

Despite the slow erosion of my sense
of self as moral being, I am happy
paying for the services I'm given.
My rooms are lit electrically. My
house is heated. And in the middle
of a heated moment, arguing bills,
I think how nice it is: the luxury
of fighting over debt, and suddenly
I find myself indebted to the people
I have never met, those murdered
by the radio while I drive my kids
to school. I turn the volume down
so they can't hear how much we
owe, or tune in to the lulling sound
that's washing between stations.

IMMORTALITY ODE

I'm coughing into handkerchiefs
and spotting blood and loving it.
No, honestly, I bring up nothing
useful, but double-check that
I'm not ailing. I'm rather pale
around the cheeks, the temples,
like one who gathers leeches
in a bleak romantic vision, who
wears his trousers rolled and
wades into a pool upon the moor
to roil the waters with his staff,
then stands there, monolithic,
baiting suckers with his legs.
He comes ashore to pluck them
one-by-one: a solitary reaper
harvesting the field, himself.
Later on, he'll hawk them
to some quack who draws
plethora—a nasty case of
humours-out-of-whack.
This isn't funny. Trust
me. I love my life,
and want to live it,
more or less.

SHELL

It may be that the laws of physics
can prove this sea is nothing more
than white noise lisping in a shell,

a vacancy now leased to ambient
sound that mimics surf—the rush
of waves arriving on a beach—

but I will feel it washing over
me as cold, a dreadful certainty
that flushes wonder from its home.

The murk is where I like to be,
the depths at which unheard of
species, grotesque lamps for eyes,

can lurk beneath the range of our
machines. I like it when an ROV
gets stuck while trying to dredge

up treasure from an ancient wreck
and surfaces with nothing but
some scuff marks on its shiny hull.

I like to think that somewhere in
the dark there is an old clay cup,
not even chipped, still bearing

maker's mark in florid script—
a holy object nestled in the silt
beside a coral crown; a sword

so furred with barnacles it looks
more like a gem-encrusted wand,
its magic now forgotten by us all.

So I hold this shell as I would hold
a phone, on hearing that my friend
has died—not ready to believe it yet,

too awed by how a distant grief has
travelled all the way to me in waves:
a shushing that's supposed to soothe.

AS YOU WERE

No matter how much tar-black muck
from a palm-sized screw-top tin
I scooped up with that yellow rag,
no matter how frantically I buffed
the armoured toes, my boots
(straight-laced, standard issue)
stayed dull as rubber soles.
Light landed on their surface
and surrendered, died in combat,
or deserted. The older kids, long ago
enlisted in the local cadet corps
(2415 Gonzaga, *Semper Magis*),
had polished theirs to mirrors.
Bow your head from attention's
rod posture and you'd see yourself
reflected hazily at roll call,
convex portrait of a soldier
framed by gymnasium lights.
Or *they* would; if I looked down
into the murk of what I'd done,
I only saw their faces staring straight
ahead like statuary, monumental
in their postures as if posted
on a marble plinth. They stood
for something, so they fell
in step. A row of flags on pikes
denoted all of us. The drums
marked time to quantify a loss.

FORT

Never a house but a fortification
we shaped from shapeless
mounds heaped by the plow,
as if the template for violent
conflict was all we knew.
And knowing nothing better,
we packed snow to form
a perimeter wall that grew
steadily with each handful
deposited and patted down,
homemade mittens crusted
with the mortar of our making.

The streetlights all lit up
as dusk set in and found us
pleased with what we'd built:
protection against come-what-
may, a structure to repel
the vague, persistent sense
we had of something wanting
in. So we went home again,
and ate and went to bed
while on the hallway rad
our frozen mittens dripped,
relaxing into open hands.

HOW TO MAKE A PERFECT PAPER AIRPLANE

is a booklet that my kids produced,
including hand-drawn diagrams
and the transcript of an interview

with my ten-year-old, whose hunch
is that the landing on this flight
of stairs would be ideal for launch-

ing craft. Just days ago, in school,
he'd been annotating loose-leaf
with his awkward pencil scrawl

of words spelled out phonetically,
or columns of mathematic sums,
but now my serious, melancholy

son is focused on his prototype,
a blank page buoyed by alien design
and drifting lazily, aloft, unlike

its archetypal cousin, the angry jet
that strafed my grade six classroom
to crash against the teacher's desk,

piloted by no one. Aim is overrated.
When his plane falls short, I tell him
nothing lands where we anticipate it

will, and nothing lasts. Soon, the first
day back to school in months, he'll fly
impatiently from me as if the worst

has passed. Maybe it has. It's hard
to watch what's left our hands
continue on a steady course toward—

THE WORK OF ART

A dorm room, unadorned, is wanting
ornament, so we gather the remains
of student loans we spilled all over
George Street bars and come to this
odd gallery of greats: iconic stills
from famous films; a kitten barely
holding on, beneath the thin decree
of optimism's broad philosophy:
Hang in there! Sage advice for any
student balancing a bender
with a thousand words on Benjamin,
plus bibliography, no chaser.
There's clocks so hot they puddle
on the landscape; the self-drawn
hands of existential, self-made man;
the Lady of Shalott is sad, and
borne away on a gondola by grief;
a hundred other unframed images,
reflections of the world outside
these library stalls we toil in
like monks in a scriptorium,
attendant to the wisdom of the age.
We copy it from books because
a species thrives by reproduction—
we learned this in biology,
tenth grade. A blank page draws
the mind into a terrifying void,
before a time when art was made.
Before the prehistoric caves.
Before graffitied Roman alleyways.
Before my youngest scribed
a filigreed semblance of vines
on the dining room wall. Pacino

is the picture of a handsome,
melancholy duke whose heavy-
lidded eyes pursue us through
the gallery; Jack Nicholson has
gone insane again, and grins;
that tidy little room in Arles
has artwork hanging on its walls;
the kitten dangles from a line
because it's all there is to hold.

IN THE AGE OF MECHANICAL REPRODUCTION

I clamp these sausages with tongs
to cut all three at once, in one
smooth motion for my children who look just like me.

MUSEUM DIORAMA

These platforms are the flakes
where salted fish were fanned
like valentines unfolding
at the half to form a heart.

This tiny tub, enlarged
to human scale, was full
of livers rotting forth
a daily dose of health.

Those floats are markers
for the nets that lie
beneath the waves
created by a craft

stick dabbling epoxy,
a bay in which
cod ran so thick
boats barely made it

through. It's been vetted
by committee, so it's true.
It documents a way of life,
but obviously reduced.

SCOPE

This is a long shot,
a half-mile off,
strong easterlies
skewing the trajectory
of events,
but despite prevailing
weather conditions
(relative humidity,
bayonets of wind)
there's always a straight
line between two points:
the muzzle in the bushes
and the officer
unwinding in the darkness,
suddenly struck
by the need to smoke
a pipe and have a think
on where he aimed
and where he ended up:
stuck, mired, idly
writing home on scraps,
wanting nothing
more than hot water,
a leisurely bath—the last
thing in his head
before he lights the match.

SHOOTING THE MESSENGER

Someone's got to take the rap.
If not him, then who?
Your wife, who giggled
when he doffed his cap
and bowed so low it looked
as if he might collapse?
Your right-hand man
who sank his gaze
beneath the flagstone floor
and shuffled almost
imperceptibly one heel
against the other?
Yourself? After all,
despite the woeful tidings,
the just plain shit
news trickling
from the messenger's lips,
something in you
felt proud to catch
these intimations of the end
and cradle them;
meditate on the page
rewritten: the page fled,
taking doomsday with him.

BALLOON ANIMALS

They'll twist themselves
into almost any shape:
mice for those
who lack conviction,
giraffes for your
exotic aspirations,
humble mutts
for dull-eyed kids.

Bullied by careless keepers,
their limbs unhinge
into the purer forms:
sausage links, large
intestines, anacondas
digesting children.

SOLILOQUY

He stood in a kilt and billowing
white shirt, a local actor
whose definitive role would be
as wooden minor character
in a television crime farce
that everyone liked but me.
We were grade nine English
with its warring factions,
divided loyalties. Bra-strap
sightings excited boys bent
on conquest. The rest of us
kept watch like sentries
posted on the battlements.
Would we be tested on this?
A forest of pencils stood
poised to move on the scene
in which he paced as one
divided by two possibilities.

There is no god in heaven
and a man doing lines
in costume is the same
man in his civvies,
who courts girlfriends,
drops one day to his knee,
plots children, pays taxes,
scouts checkout lines
for the quickest means
to the end of getting home,
feeds meters to ward off
the warden's evil eye,
a ticket that foretells
the cost of spending

too long in one place,
somewhere he shouldn't be,
chafed by ill-fitting wardrobe,
pretending always otherwise.

THE DEATH OF KING ARTHUR

I'm sixteen and trying to pull
a sword out of a stone,

dreaming of this girl I know
whose skirt is silken drapery

that conceals the holy grail.
I hide inside myself sometimes

and pull the visor down
to see the world through slits,

battles going on outside
the safety of my helmet.

OUR MISSY

At the periphery of our vision, she
circled her own notion of a home:
span of five backyards where juncos
flocked to a feeder's scattered seed,
mice commuted from abandoned
lots to trespass in our basement via
cracks in the foundation. We'd see
her from afar, still as a decoy bird
of prey deflecting city pigeons,
look locked on a host of starlings
creaking in the trees. Distance made her
other, self-contained, an element
unrelated to puss lolling in a sunbeam
on our kitchen floor, puss licking
our toddler's toes, puss, impassive
at our picture window, watching dogs
stop to water the border strip of lawn
between our fence and the sidewalk.
Which version was more true? Neither
here nor there, I guess, now she's gone.

MIDWINTER

I had come here for perfection
    rarely seen outside ideal forms,
a department store's stark vision
    of a fir tree flocked with snow,
its branches full, symmetrical;
    not this twisted, hunchbacked
forest-denizen in a dark copse
    of deadfall and rot, bog-water
spewing from a gash in the ice
    crust. At its base, the bole had
divided into twins—like two
    words of a common root, long

    since grown apart in meaning.
I thought of propping both up, in
    the corner of our living room,
lop-sided boughs now balanced
    by my children's homemade
ornaments—which I can't help
    but love in spite of their misshapenness.
The chainsaw snarled and rattled
    off old grievances. It didn't
seem to matter what I chose, all
    things being equal. I cut this
path to see what I will live with.

AUBADE

To keep your sleeping daughter from waking
to a stranger in your bed, you had me
leave. I dressed. We kissed. I left,
now thrust into cliché, the newly minted
city we grew up in. Those corbels!
That crumbling façade! The patchy
maples marrying the chapel's parking lot!

Larkin had it cold, I expect. We all end up
alone at dawn, decoding from the darkness
furnished rooms—an antique dresser, open-
mawed; chair-back draped with molted skin;
our closet's closely nestled selves—awaiting
an appointment that we dread. I'll be happy
come the morning if we stay here until then.

ROAD TRIP

With not much more than gas
and stacks of compact discs,
a tote bag full of snacks,
we set out on the highway,
the hero of unknown origin,
his companion riding
shotgun: the wizened sage,
a font burbling old adages,
folk wisdom on every page.
As far as quests go, it was
pedestrian. We drank a lot
and paid too much for what
we drank; arrived, in time,
at understanding all of it,
the text beneath the text—
a revelation that flagged
us down beside a billboard
advertising guided tours,
hitched a ride some miles,
then took its leave at a motel
where we stopped to rest.

It kept happening: Three times
we ferried it across a quiet
stretch of countryside,
unpeopled but for us, until,
while fixing day-old coffee
at a rundown crossroads
station that had no clear
analogy on our map, it slipped
out back and left for good.
So we watched the exits
disappear into the past

tense of our rear-view
mirror, hoping for another
glimpse of what we'd seen,
but there was nothing.
We drifted to the shoulder,
waiting out a column of
impatient cars that lurched
into the other lane to pass,
heedless of what might be
barrelling from the blind
hill up ahead. And happier
that way, I guess.

In the end, we returned
to what we knew, the same
old tropes that come at us
again, renewed, the road
signs counting down until
there's nothing left to tell.

CODA

Because I had no means
to heft my new guitar
on outings to the park
so that we all could sing
about what troubled us—
near-adults at the cusp
of a new millennium—
I threaded half a foot
of rope through two
holes bored into the box,
then knotted both ends
so they held: a thing
that I could grasp.

Summer was about to end.
School was done for good.
Things as they were
would soon be changed
into the college life: a first
real job, a different home.
The old was fading out.

I strummed whatever
chords I knew, fretting
over each flubbed note,
until at last, I hit a sound
that resonated out beyond
the borders of the park—
that sense we sometimes
have of being one
among the many parts.
It wouldn't last. I knew

that even then. I broke
a string and had to play
the night out from that gap.

ACKNOWLEDGEMENTS

Earlier versions of several poems previously appeared on/in Flahoolic: A Poetry Podcast, Newpoetry.ca, *Canadian Notes & Queries*, *GUEST*, *Luminus*, *Poetry Ireland Review*, *Riddle Fence*, *The Walrus*, *I Found It at the Movies: An Anthology of Film Poems*, and *The Next Wave: An Anthology of 21st Century Canadian Poetry*; and/or were collected in the chapbooks *Sea Legend* and *Skylarking*.

"The Monitor" is for Charlie, Jude, and Eleanor. "Romantic" is for Craig Francis Power. "Science Camp" is for Andrew McCall. "Skylarking" is for my mother, Patricia Callanan. "How to Make a Perfect Paper Airplane" is for Jude. "Museum Diorama" is for Mary Dalton. "Aubade" is for Andreae. "Road Trip" is for Milan Parab.

Financial support from the City of St. John's, Arts NL, and the Canada Council for the Arts was crucial during the writing and editing of these poems.

Thanks to everyone who contributed to this book, in many and various ways—especially my editor, Luke Hathaway: a new romantic in the old style.

Mark Callanan is the author of two previous poetry collections. He was one of the founding editors of the St. John's, Newfoundland-based literary journal *Riddle Fence* and co-edited *The Breakwater Book of Contemporary Newfoundland Poetry*. He lives in St. John's with his wife, poet and critic Andreae Callanan, and their four children.